All My Hearts is a hand drawn doodle book of pages to fill with your love of color.

I hope you have as much fun coloring as i did in creating this book for you. There are 17 designs, some have been duplicated and reversed in black, these you can use with gel pens on the black areas for a different effect. Another way to enjoy the designs is to follow the lines with a black marker adding your own doodles here and there, I did this on a couple of the designs and it is so much fun to see how bold and interesting they become, well i won't keep blah, blah, blah,blah,blah. Grab your crayons, colored pencils, markers, gel pens and ENJOY!'
—-D`Fleur,

Daphanie Flowers

I belong to: _____

_____

_____

_____

_____

_____

_____

_____

_____

dated:

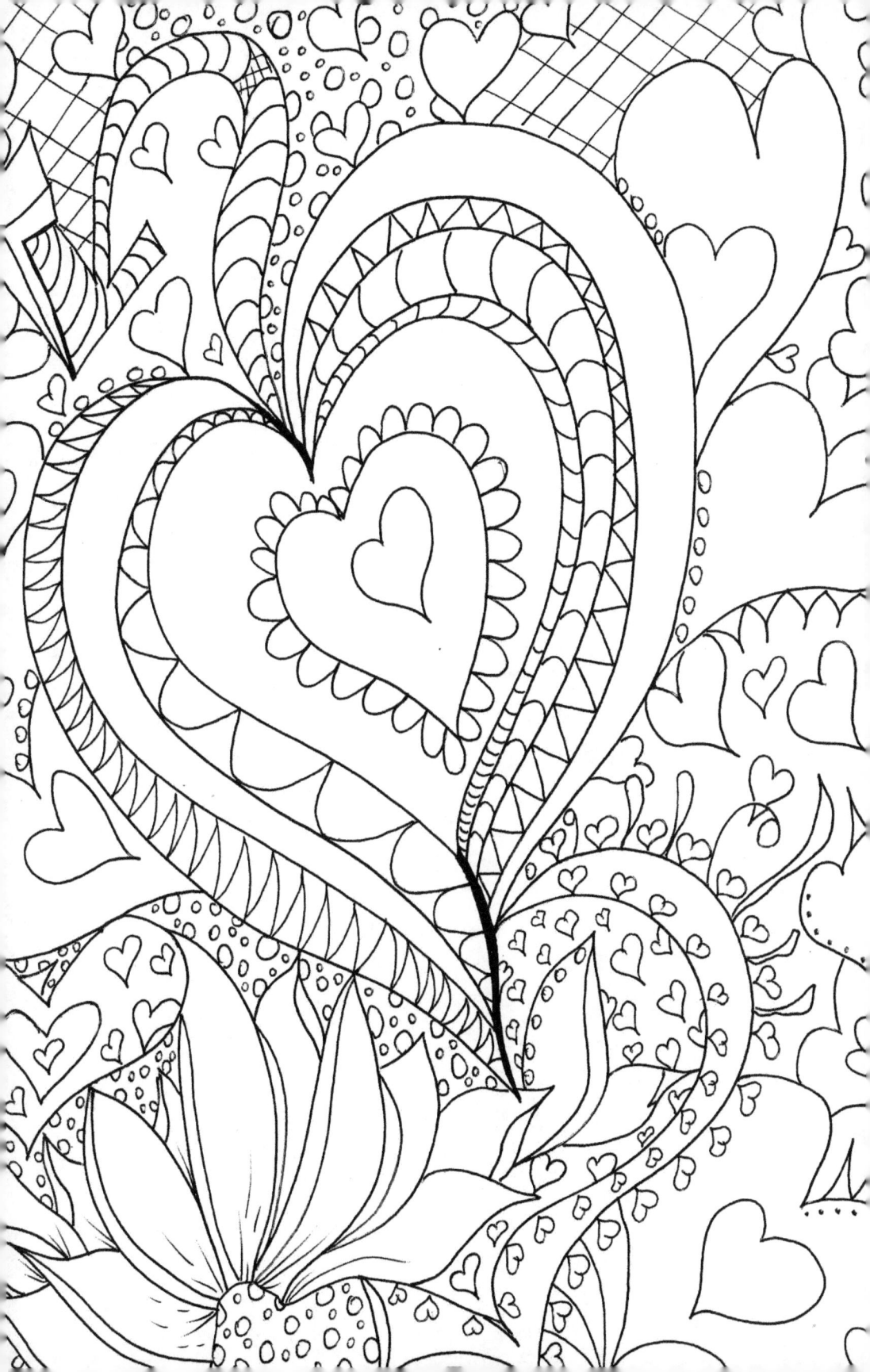

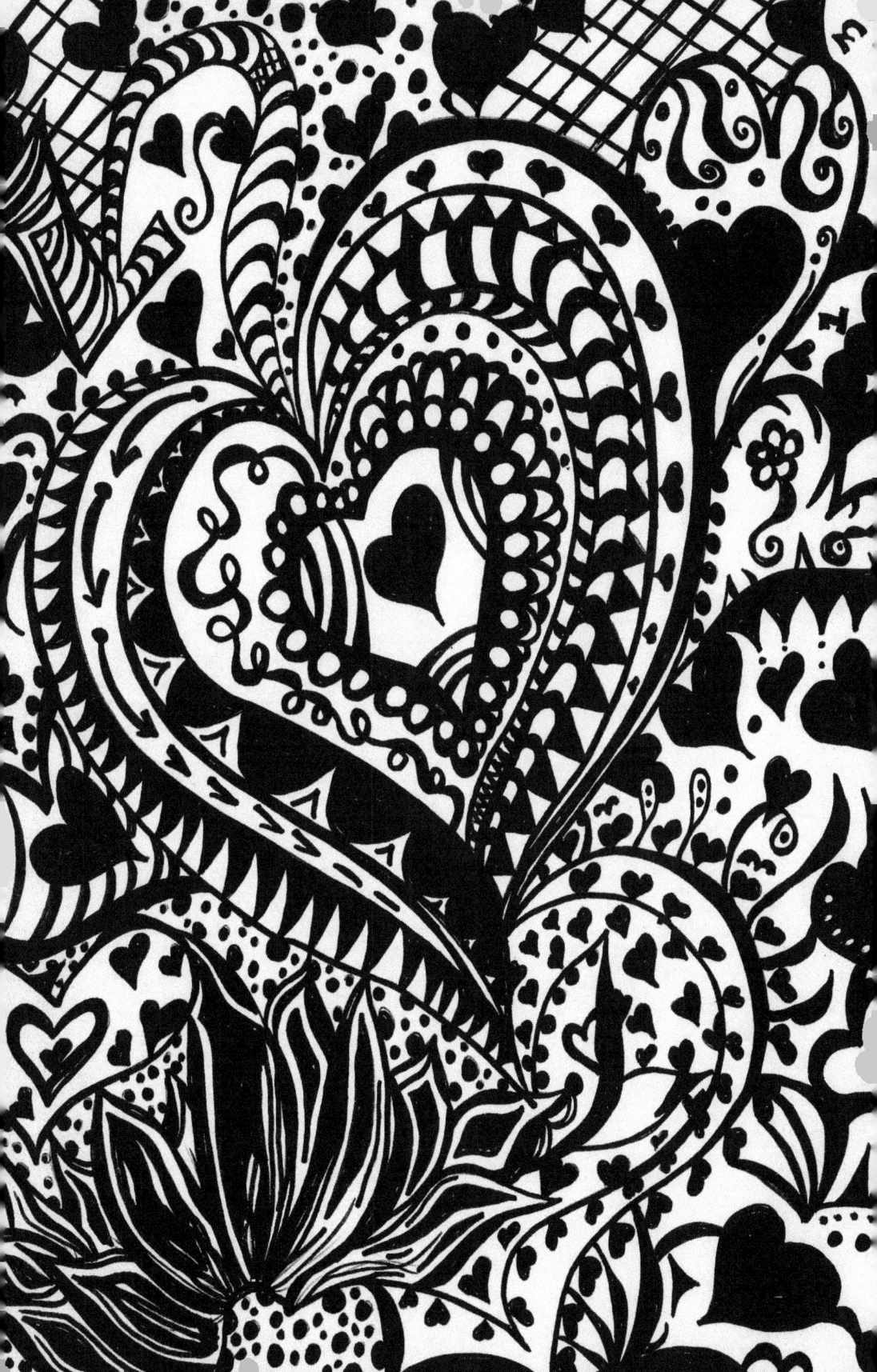

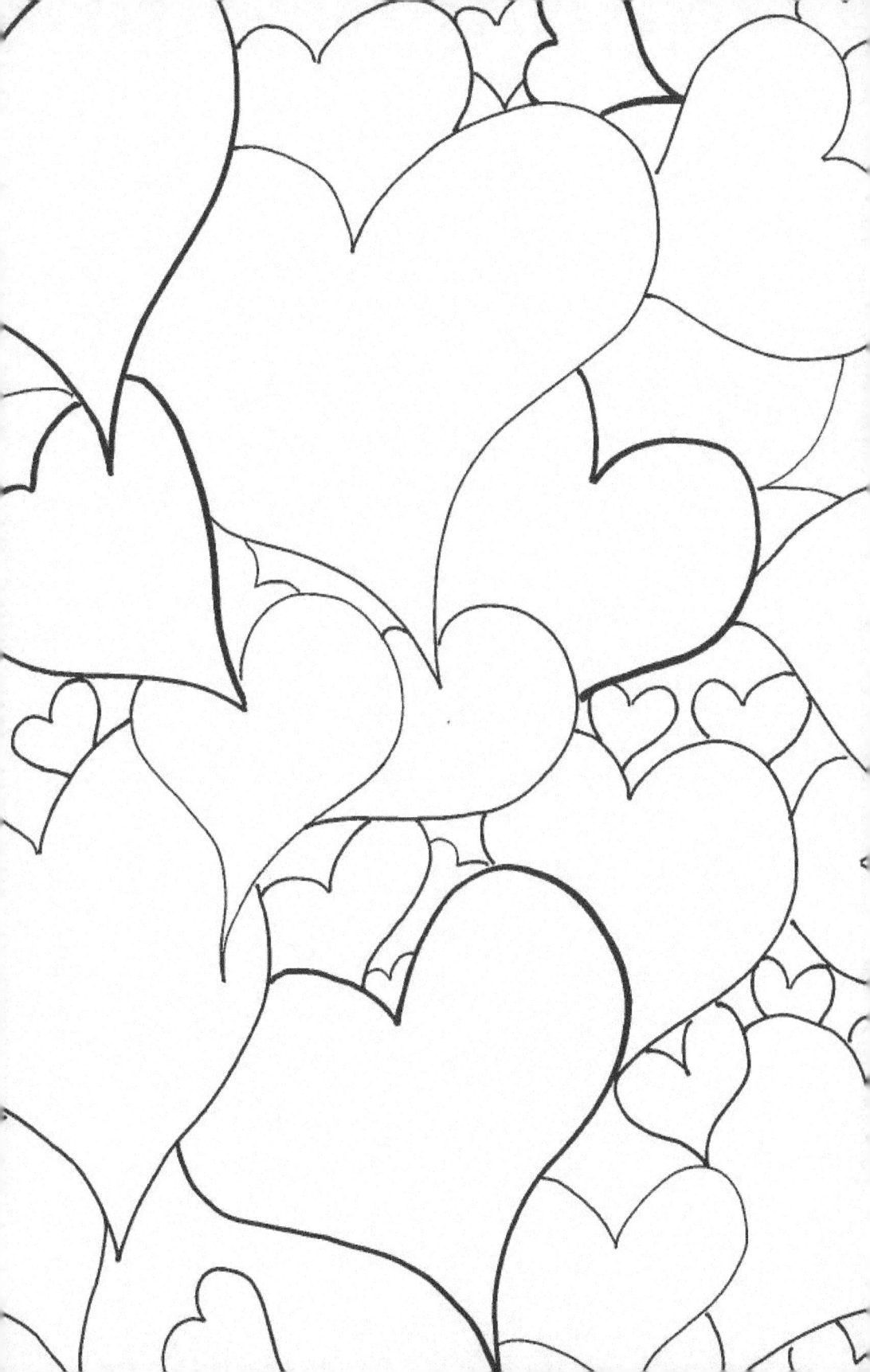

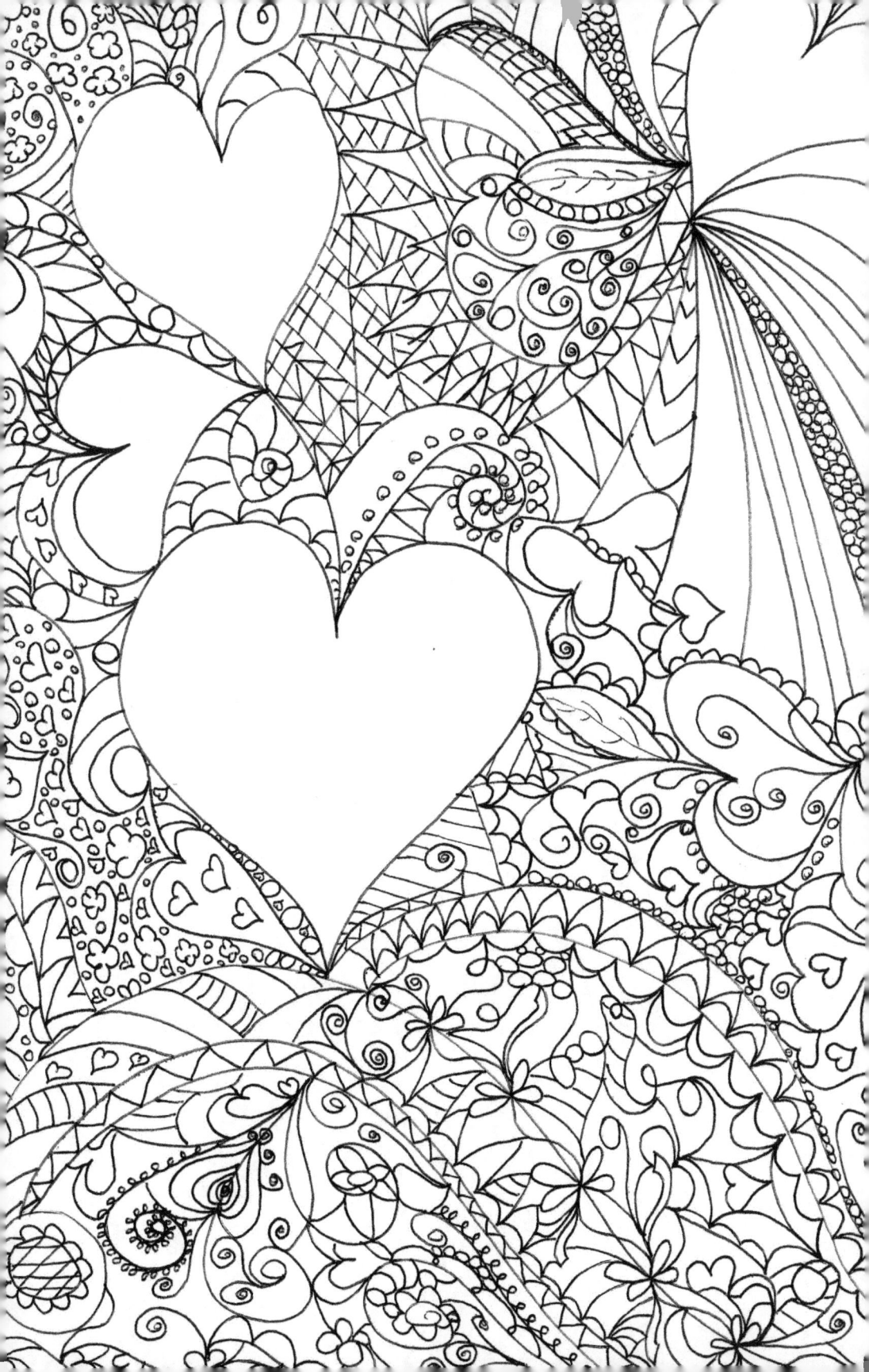

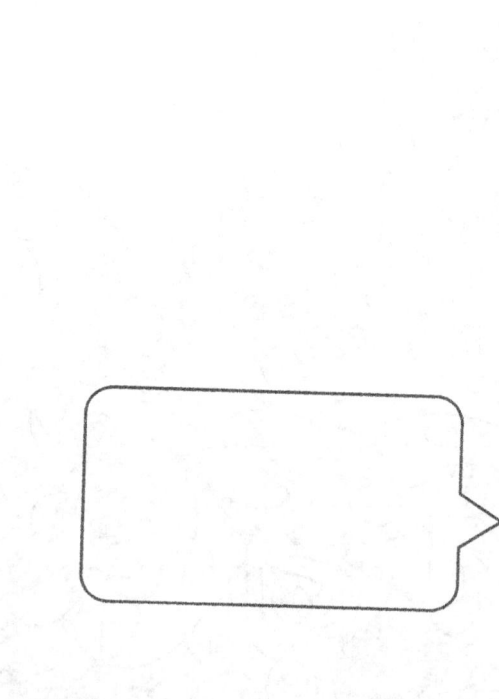

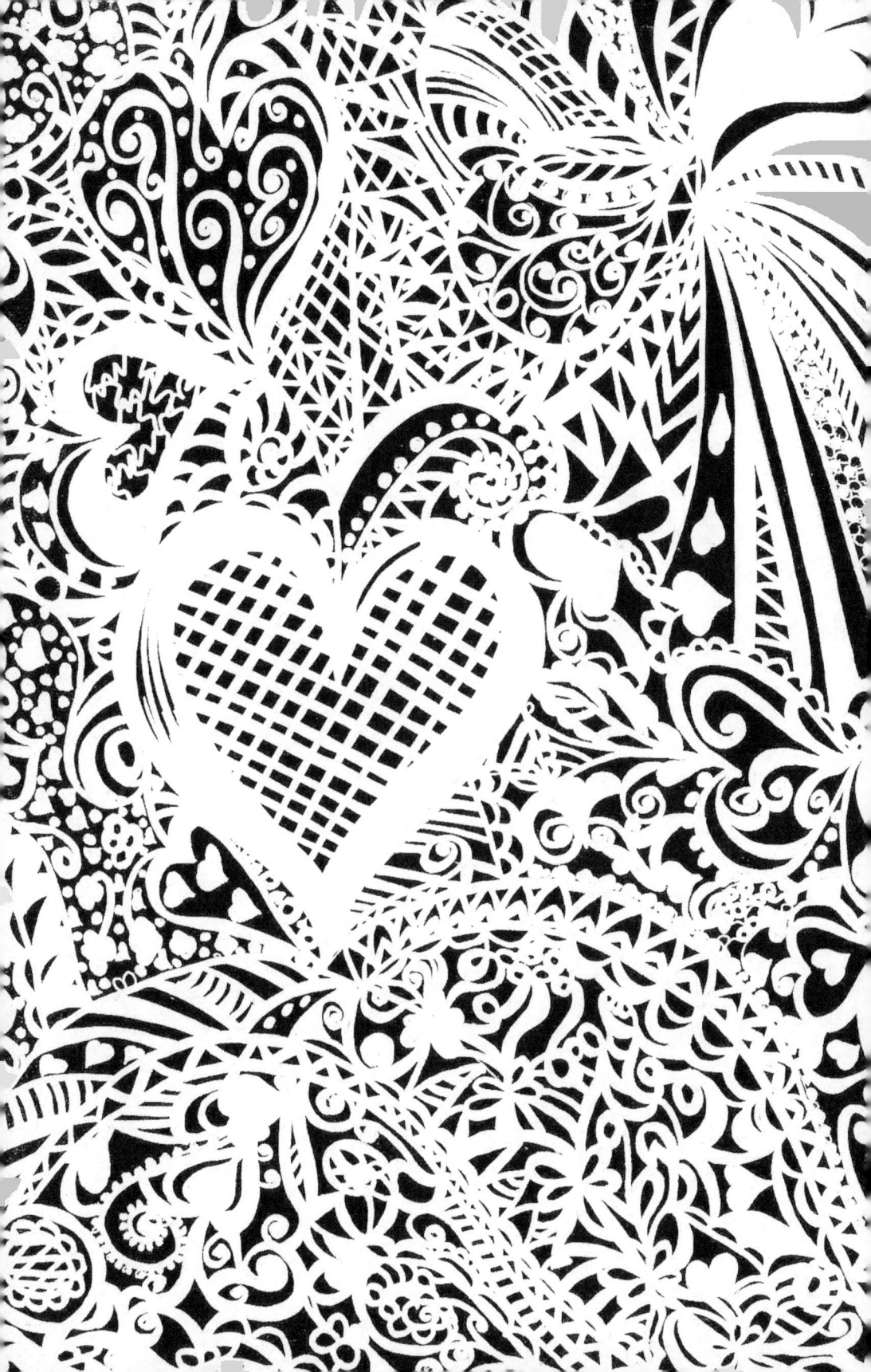

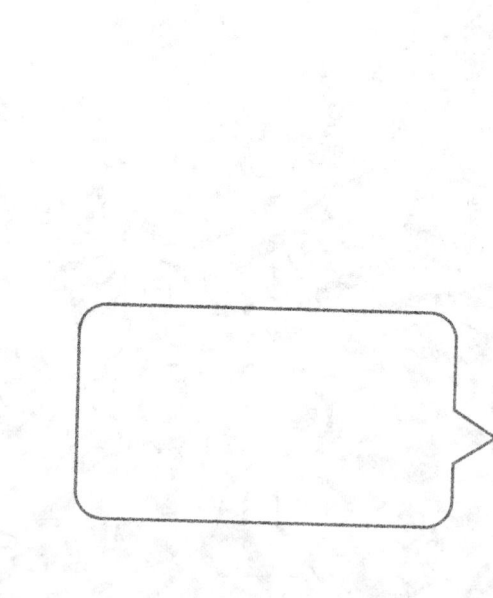

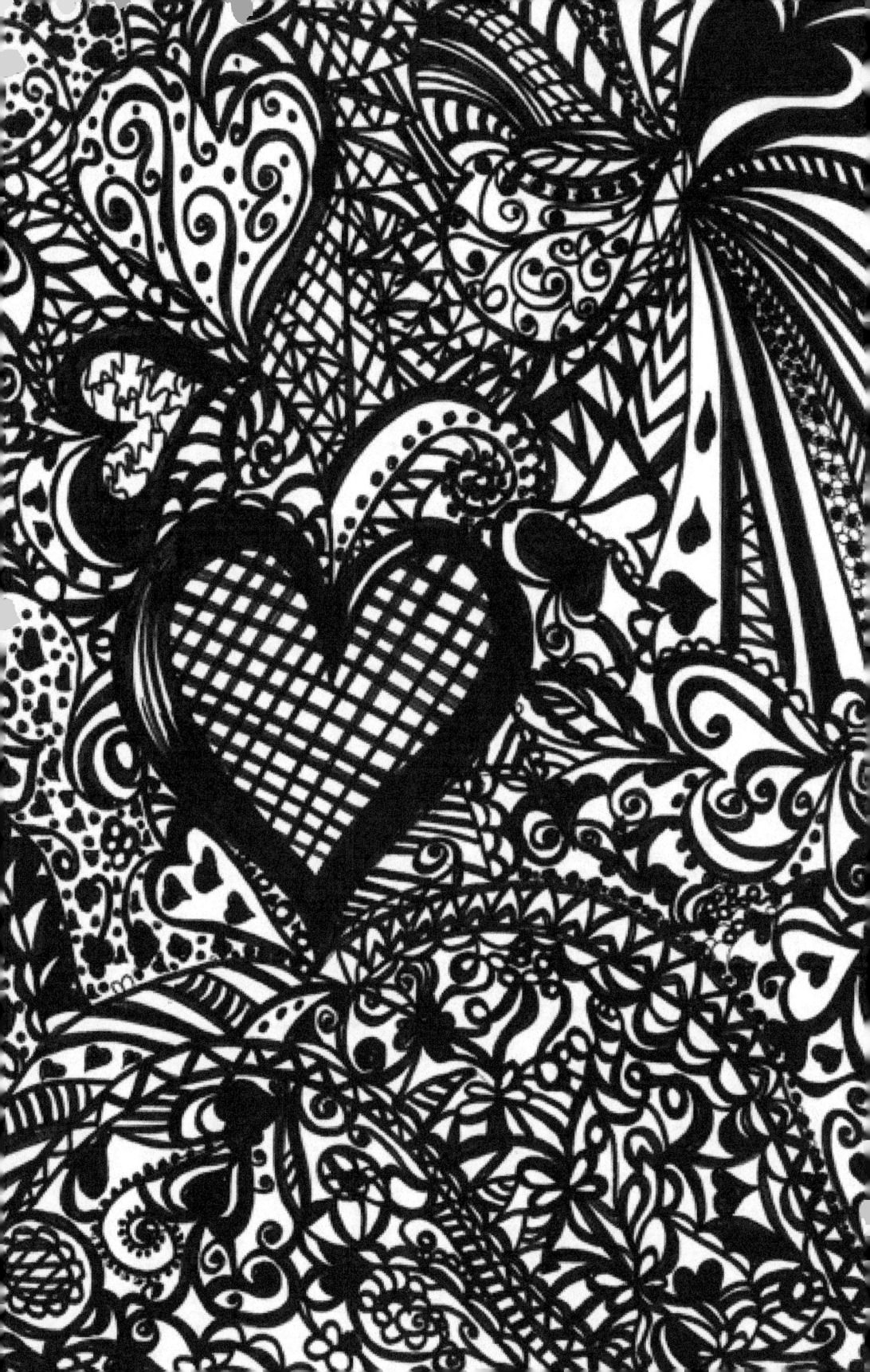

Today:

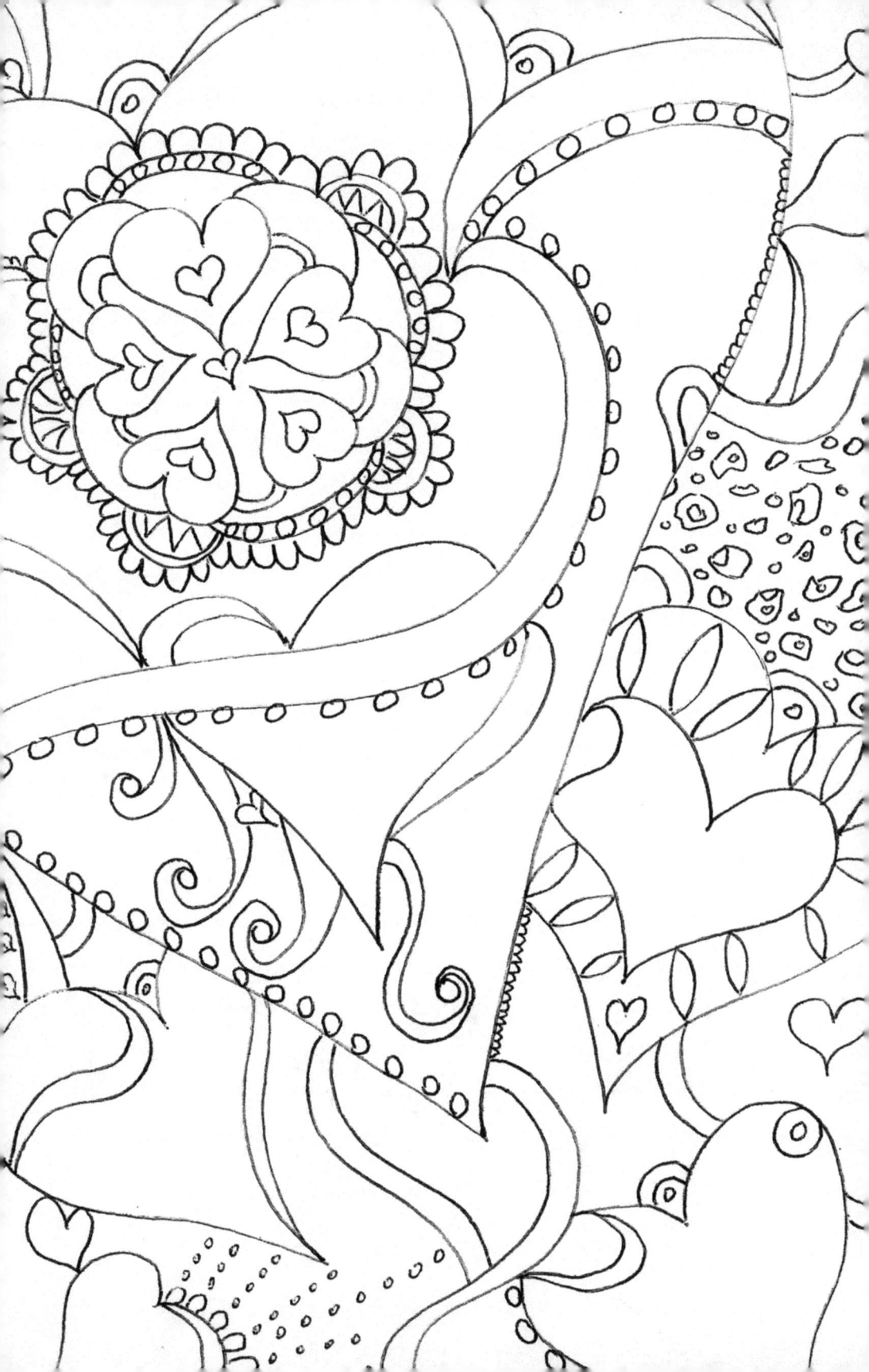

Today:

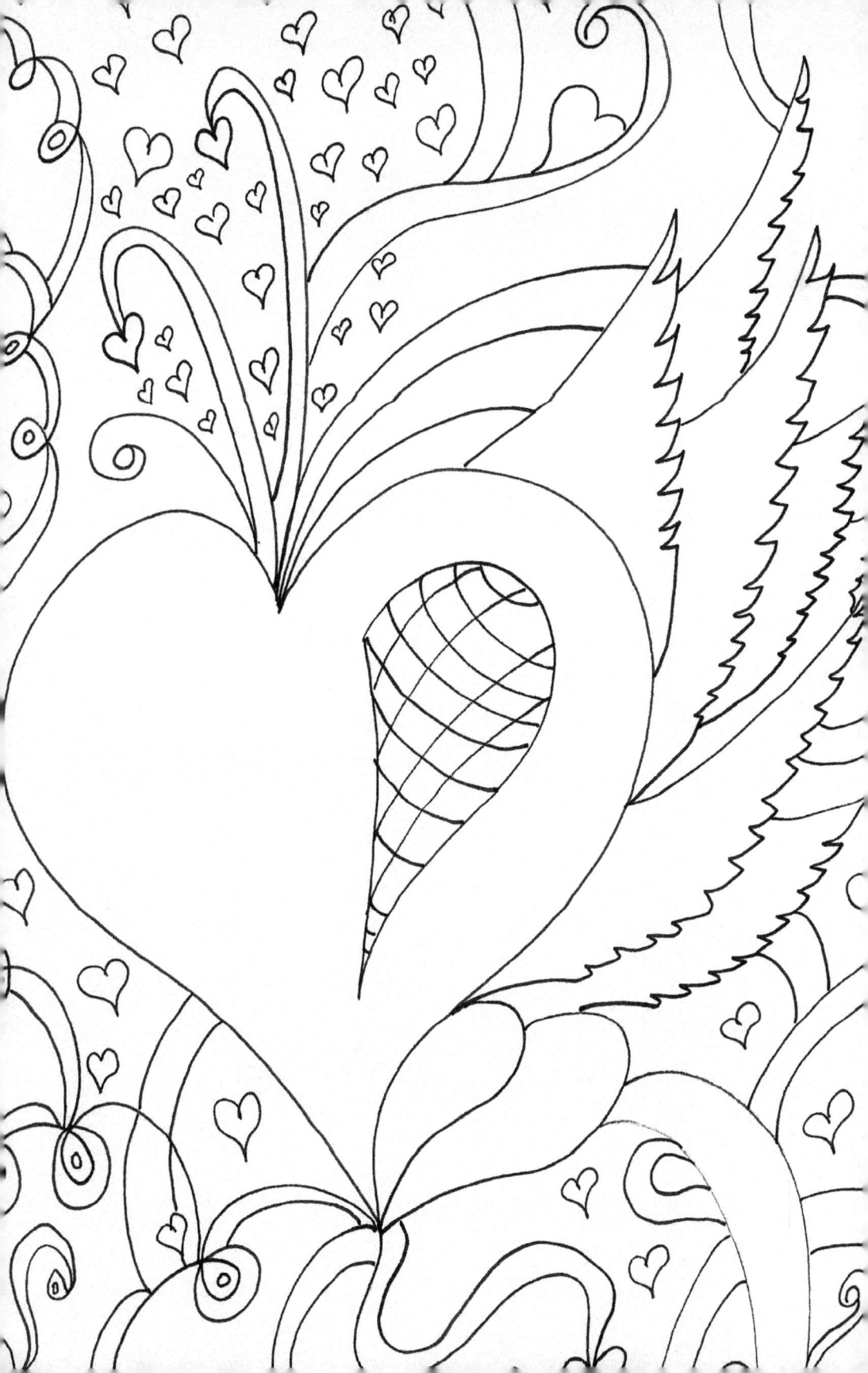

Oh yea:

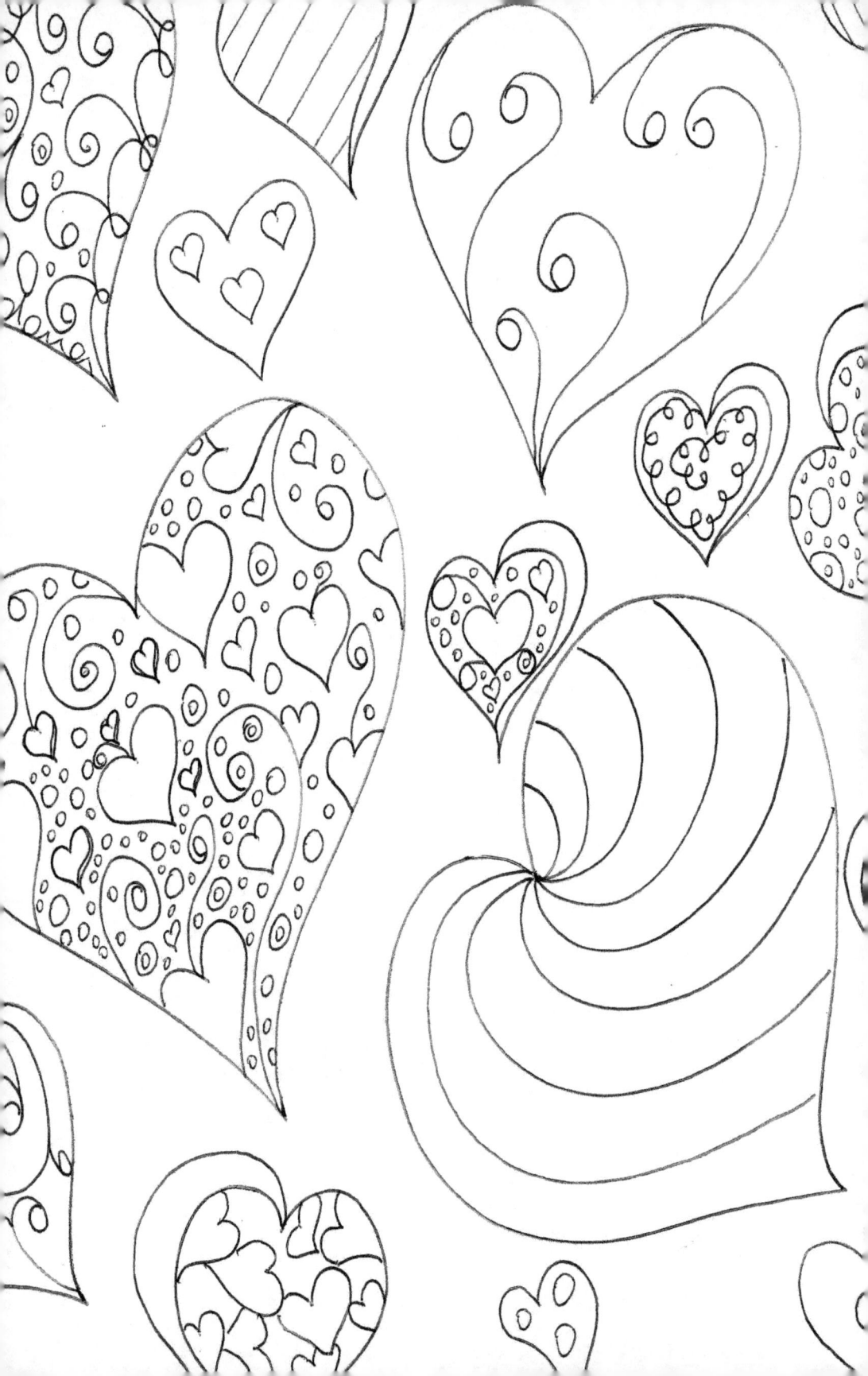

When i color

Dated:

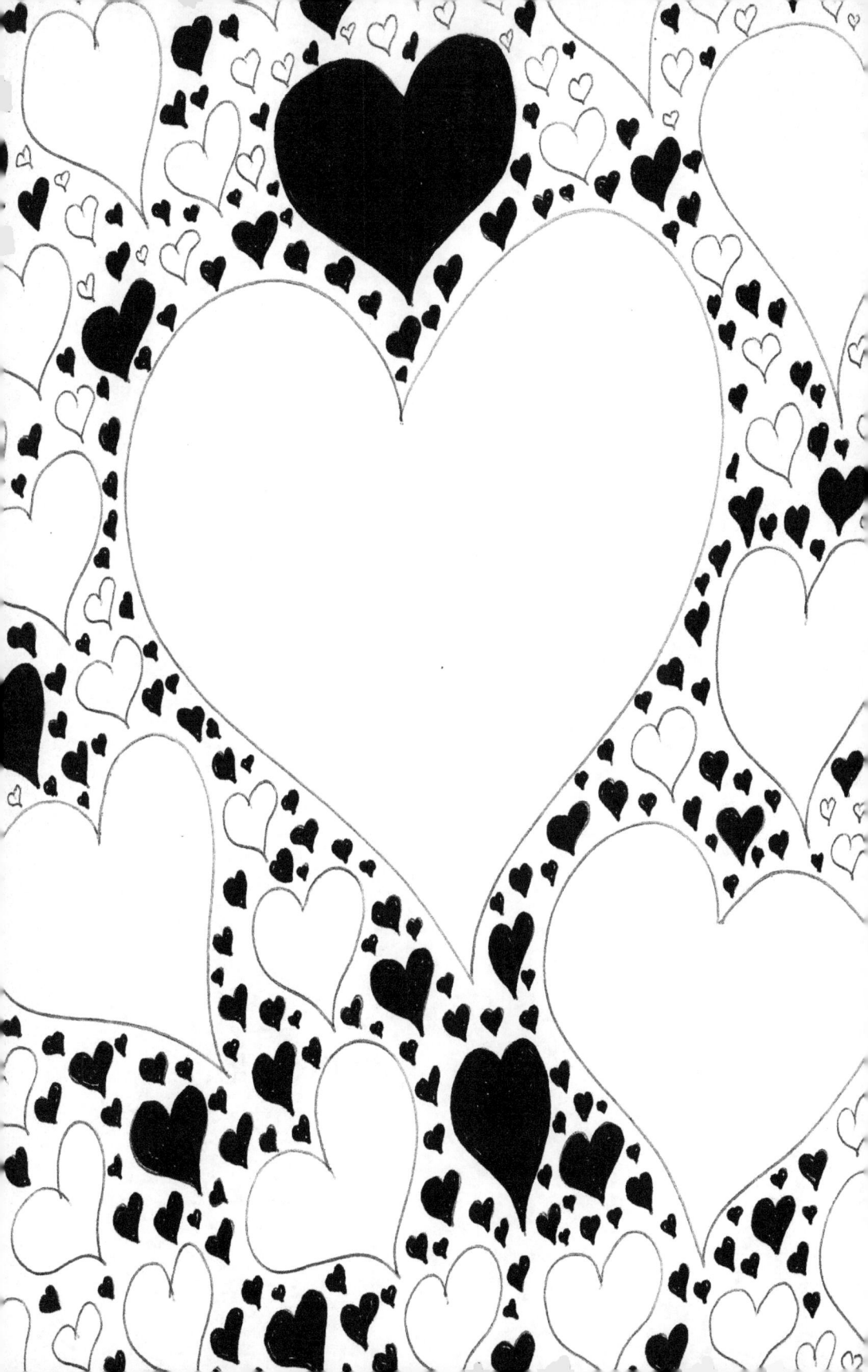

What i love

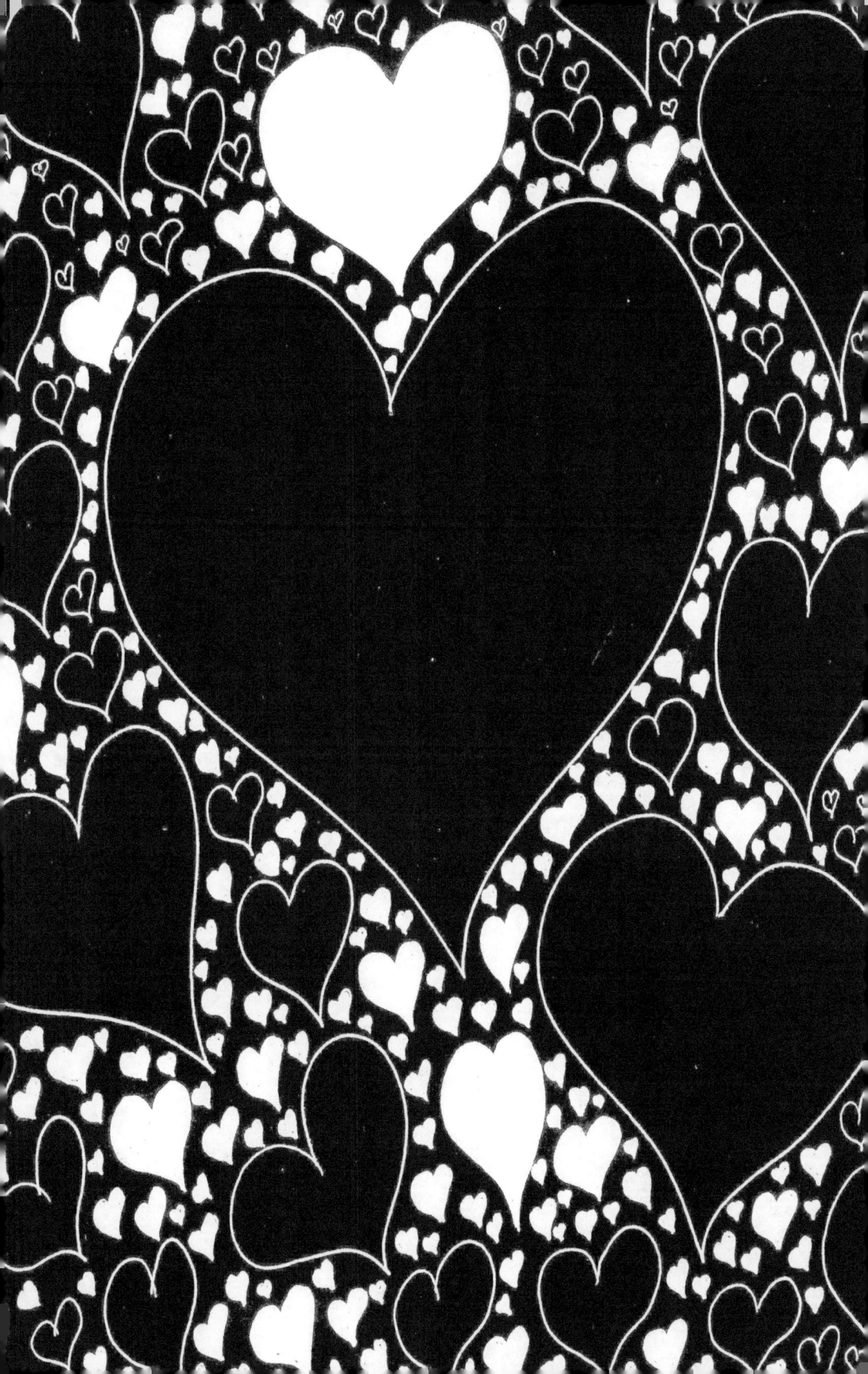

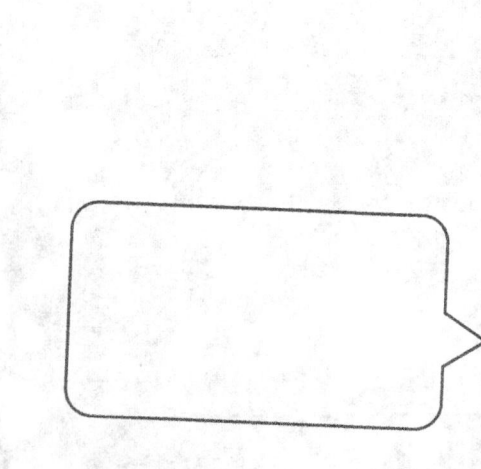

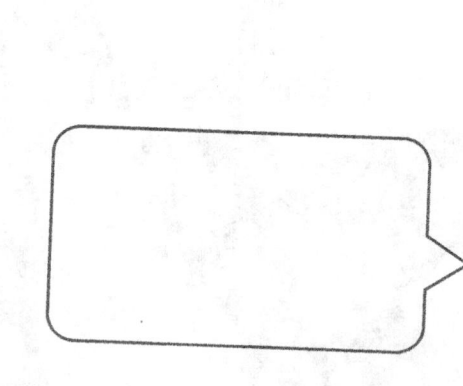

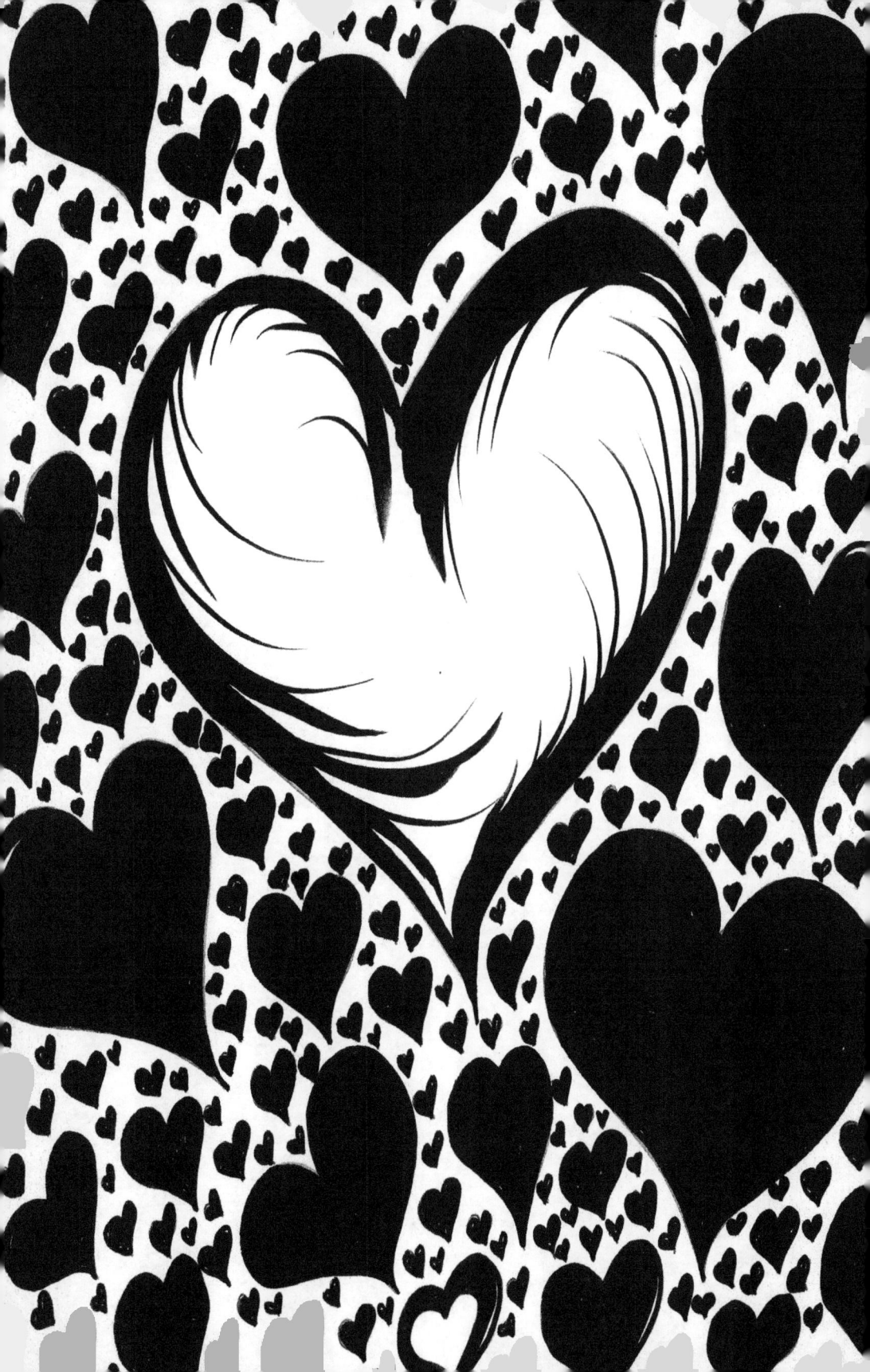

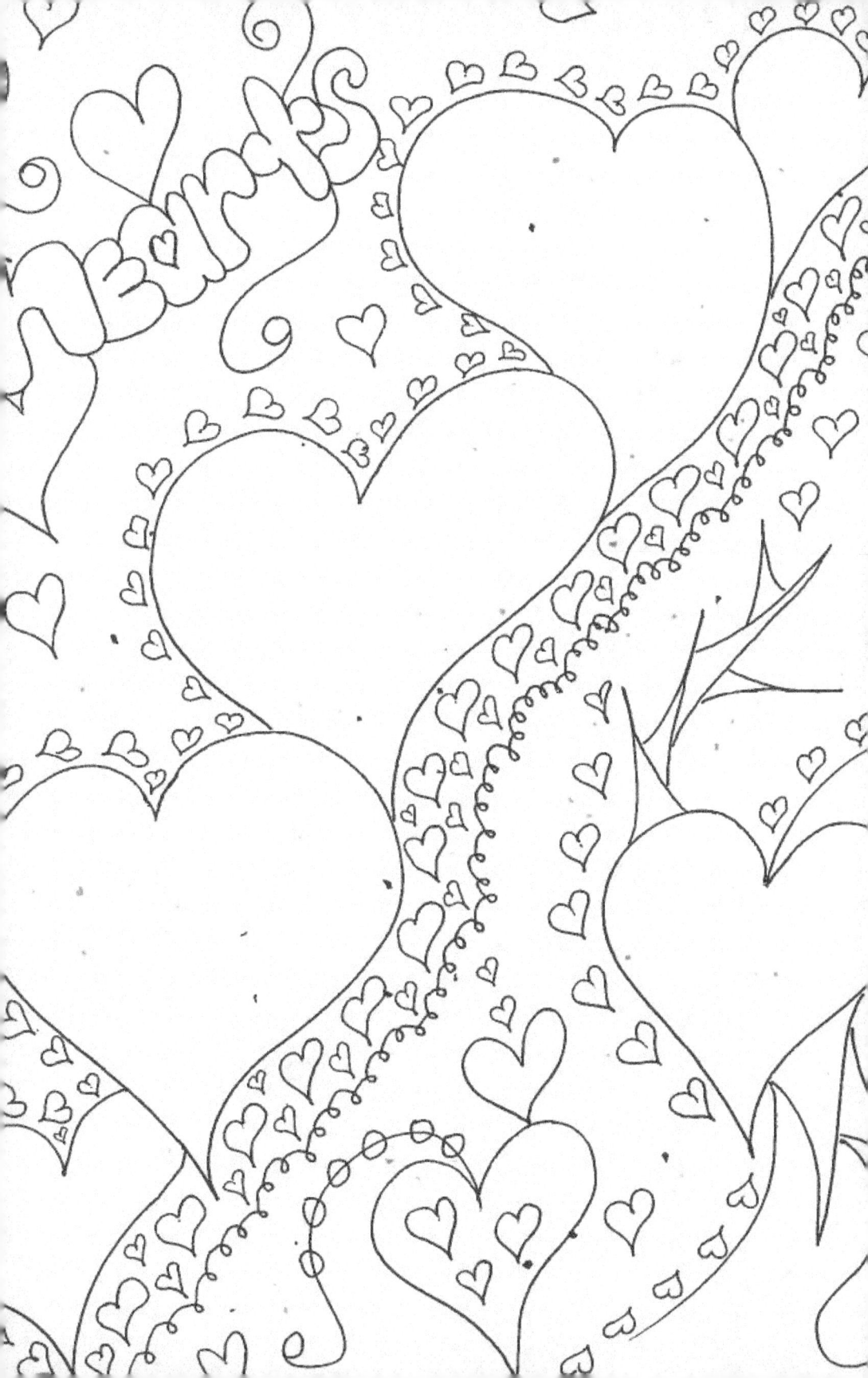

Sometimes…

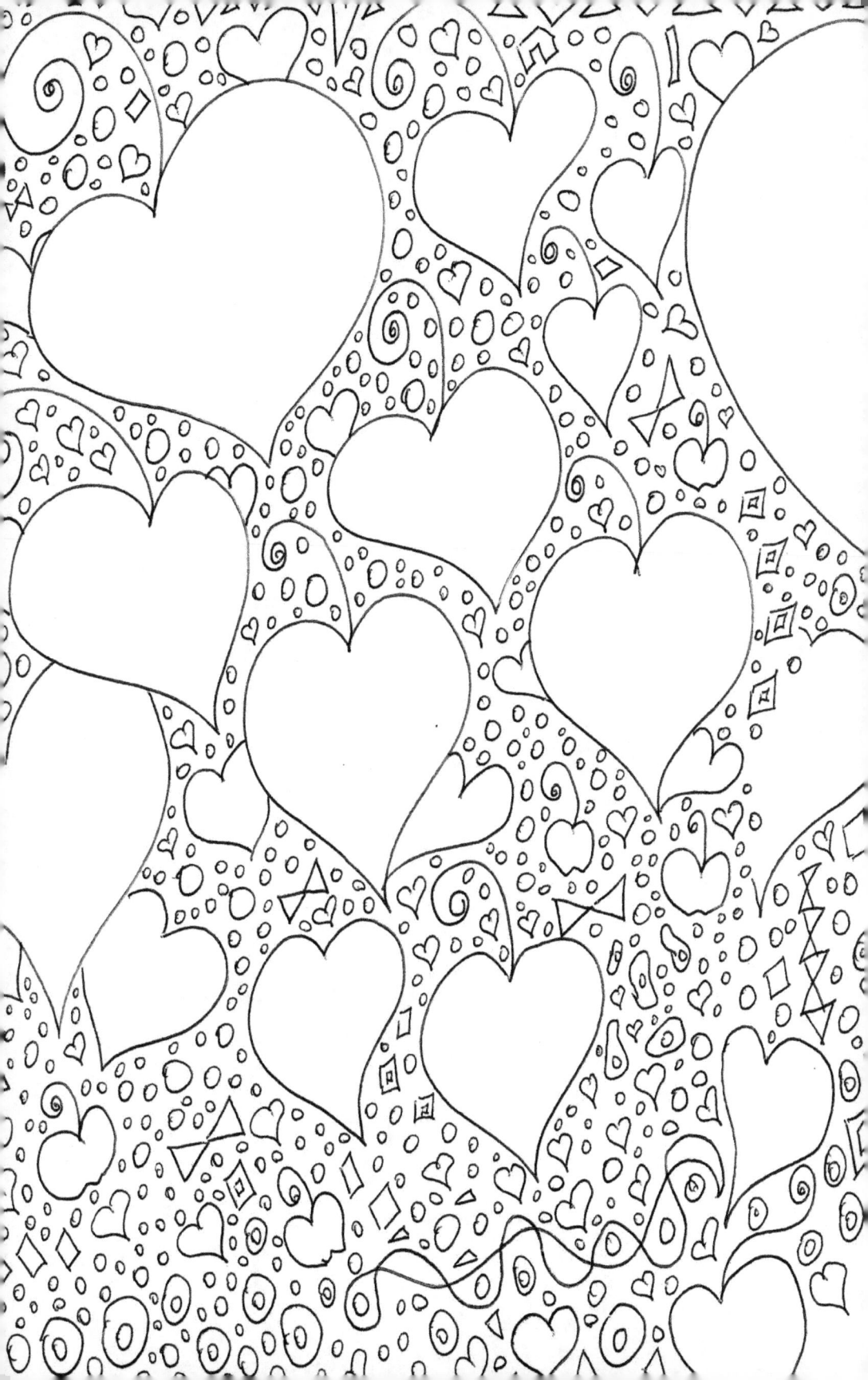

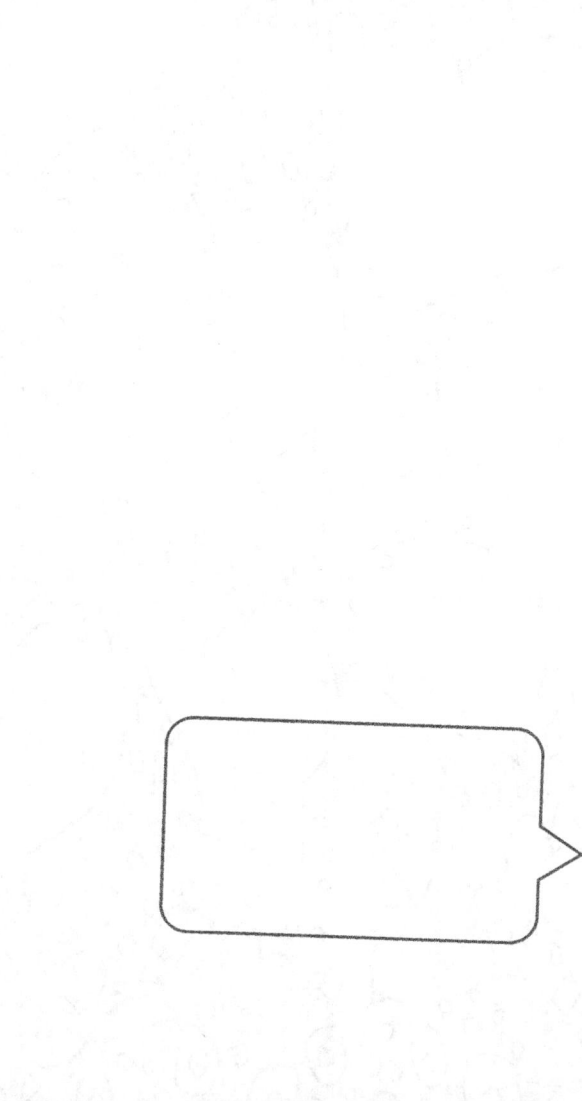

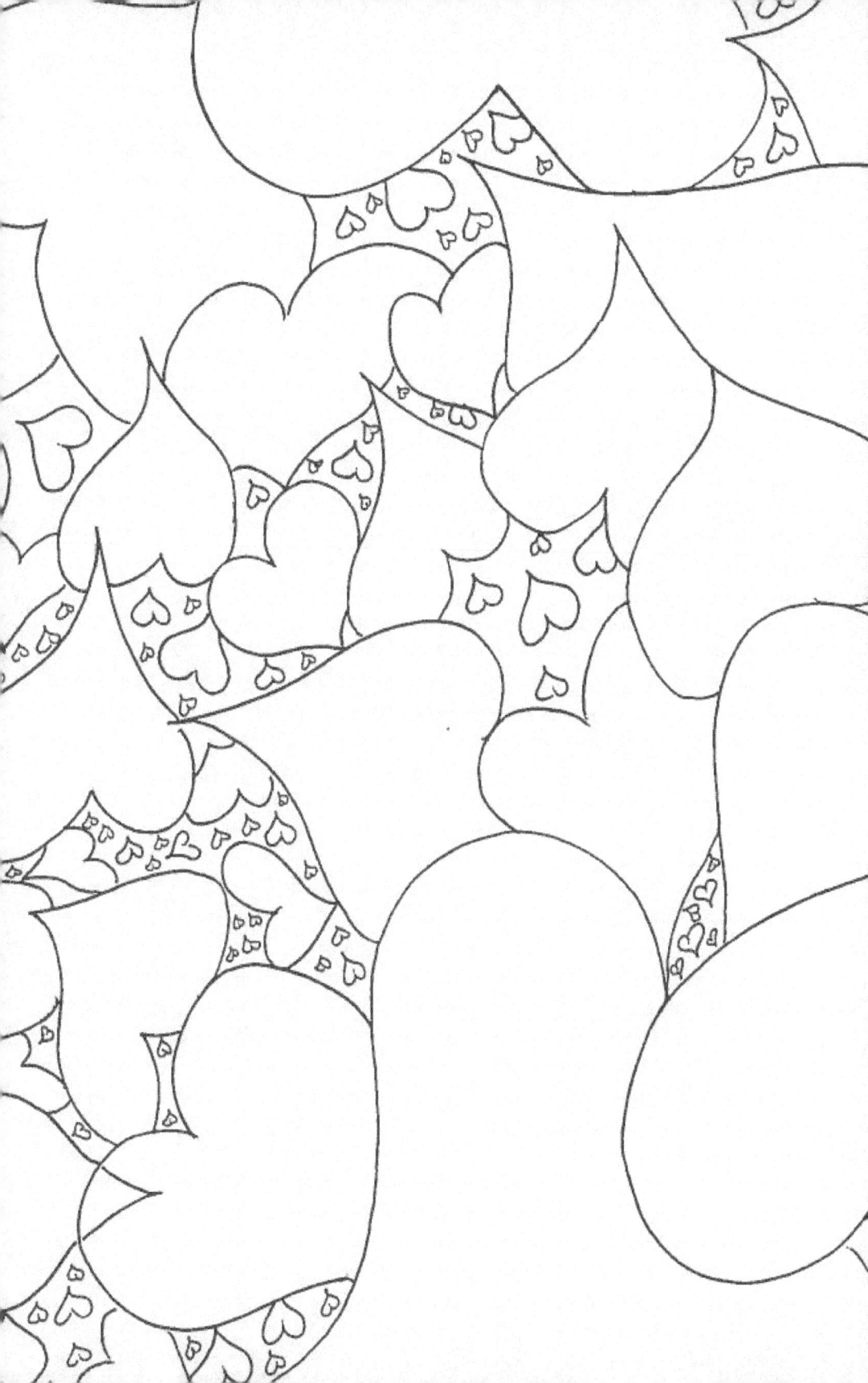

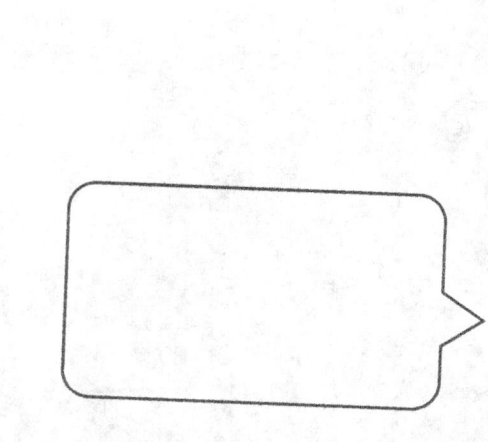

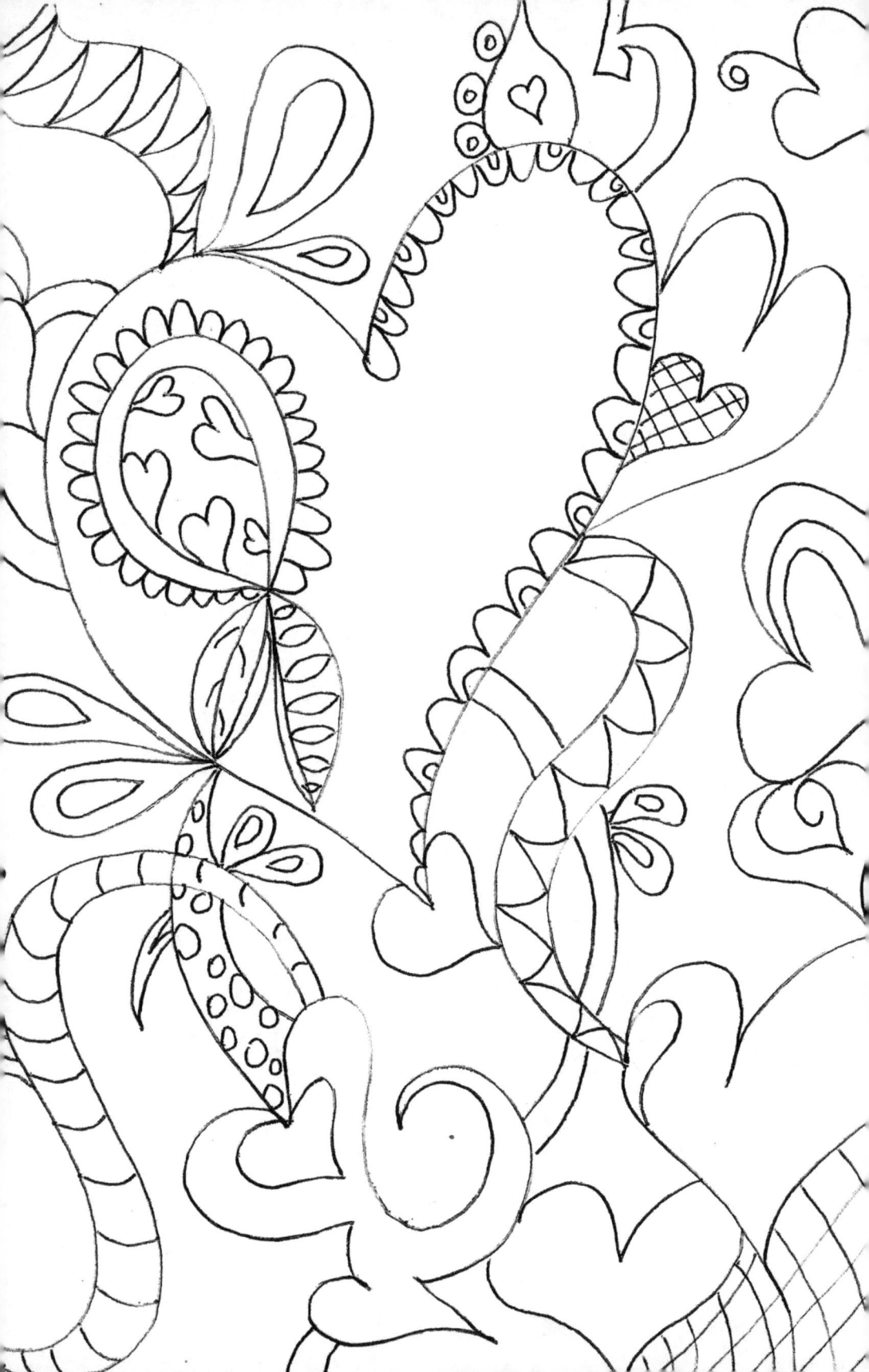

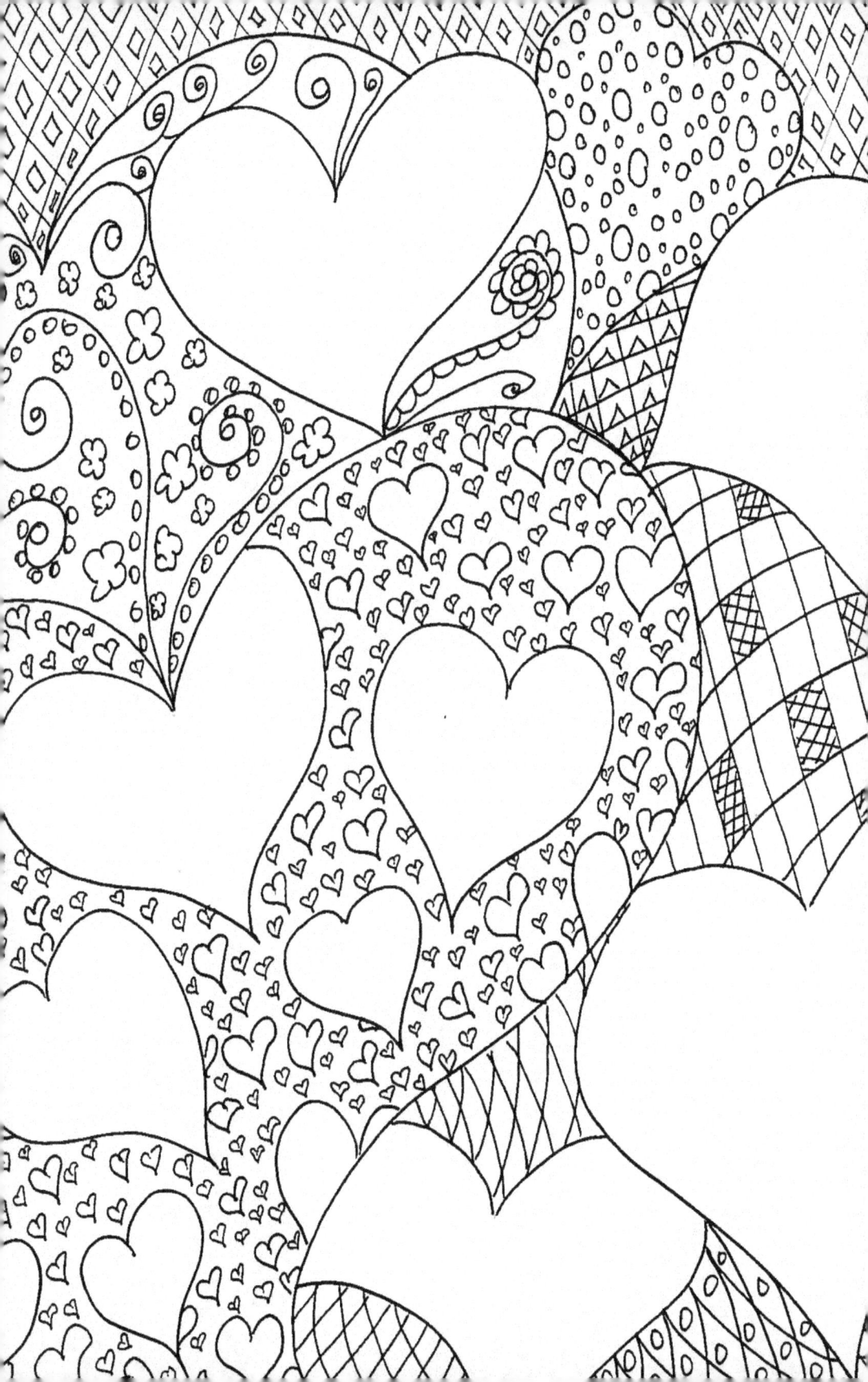

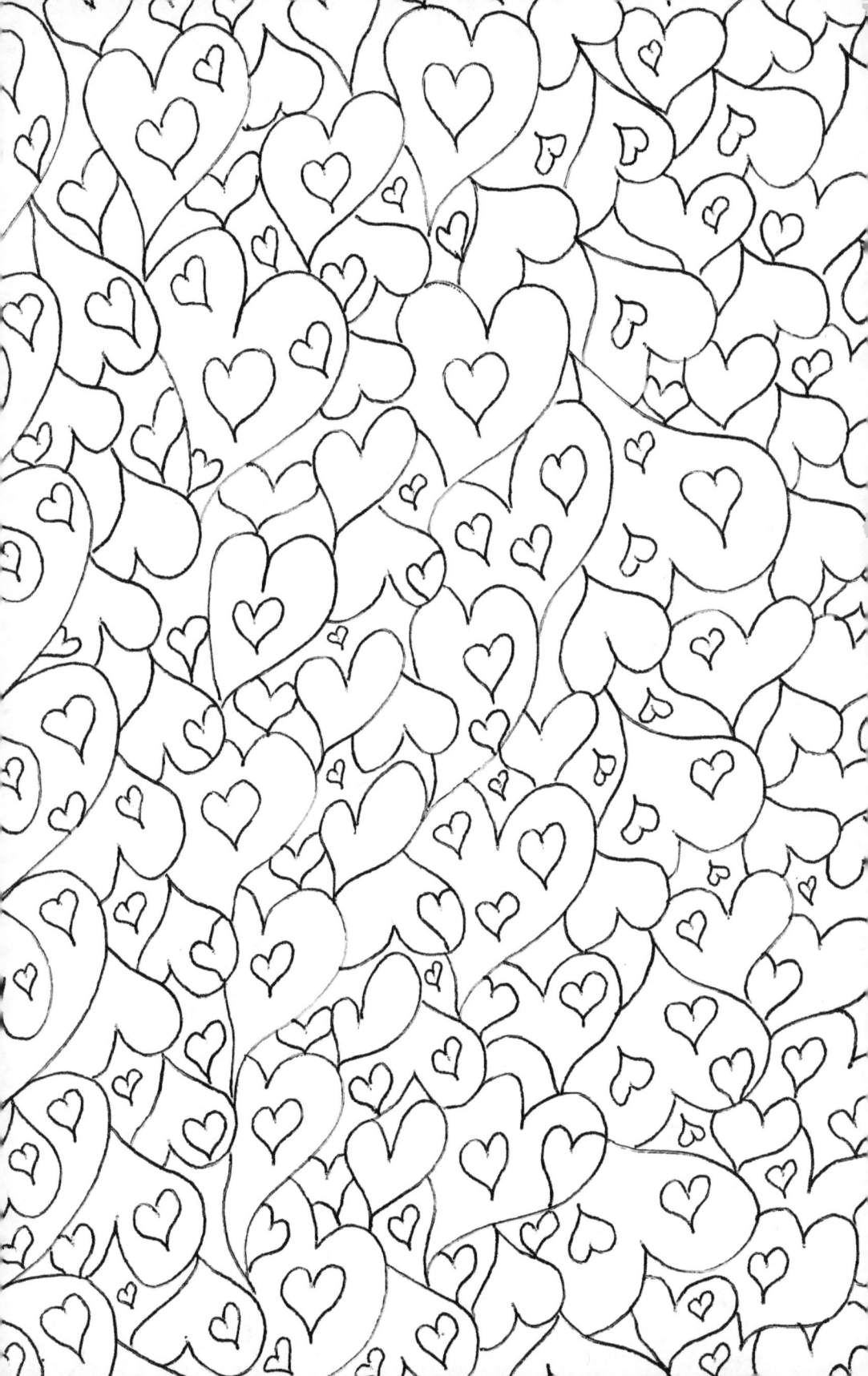

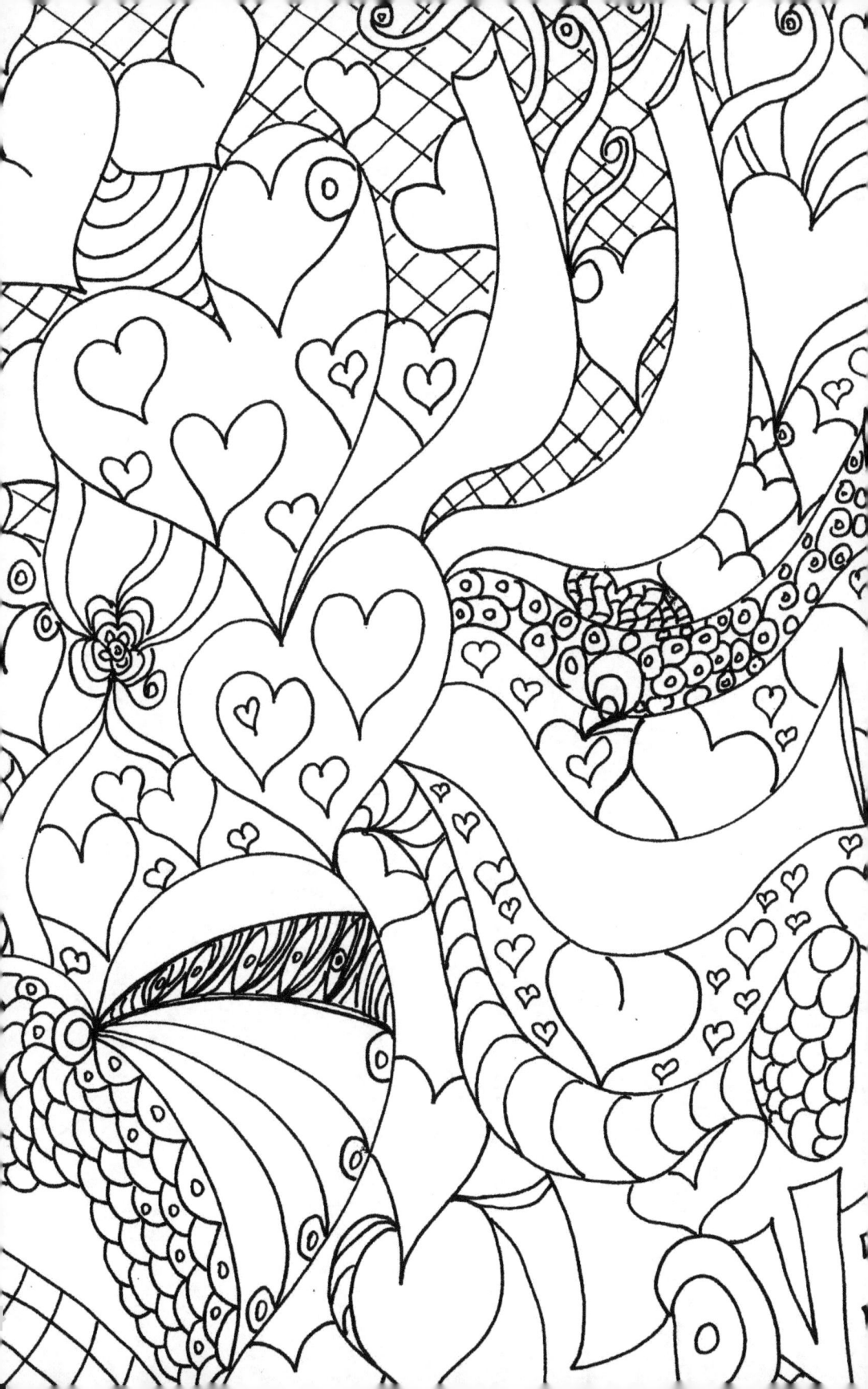

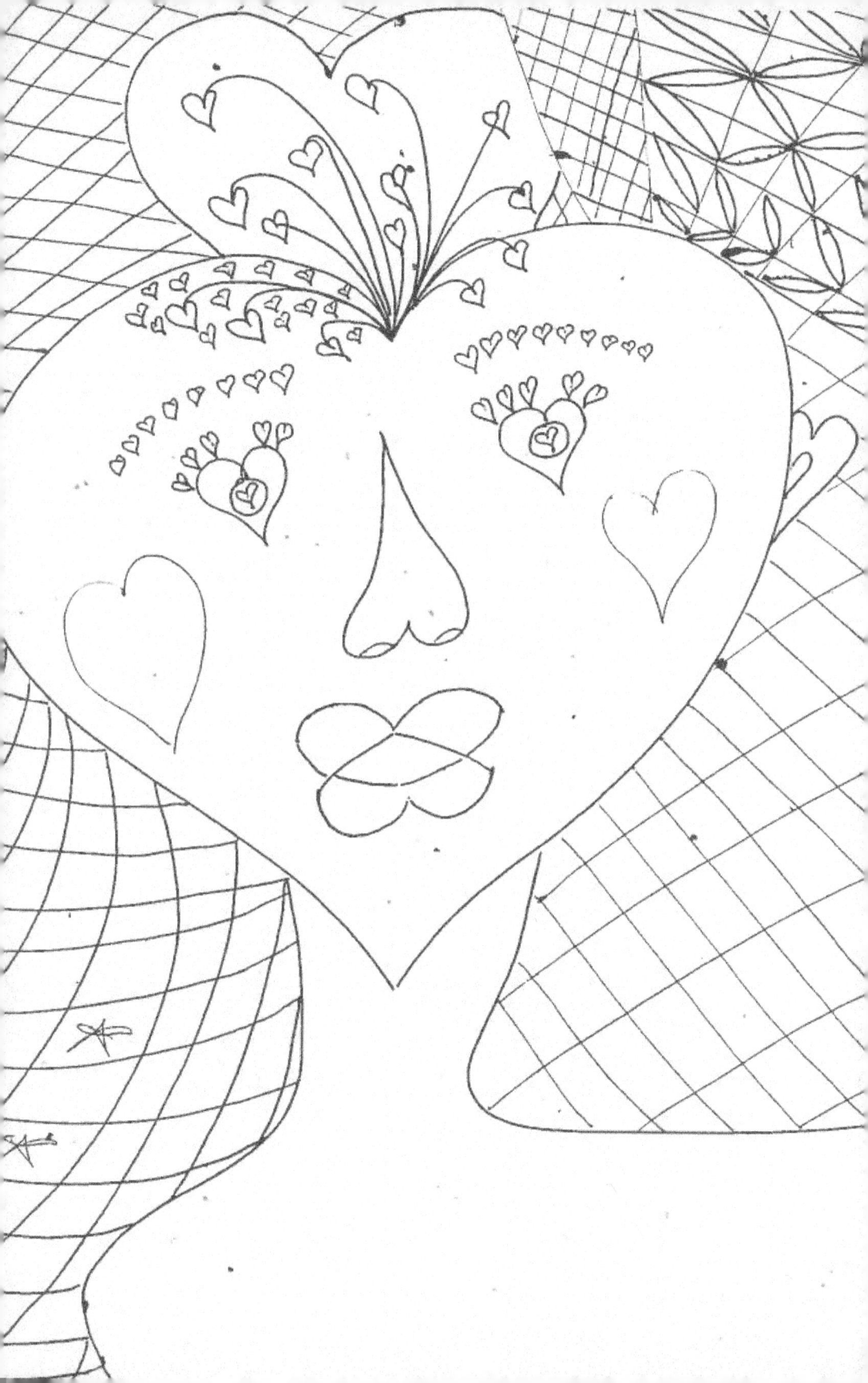

Always…

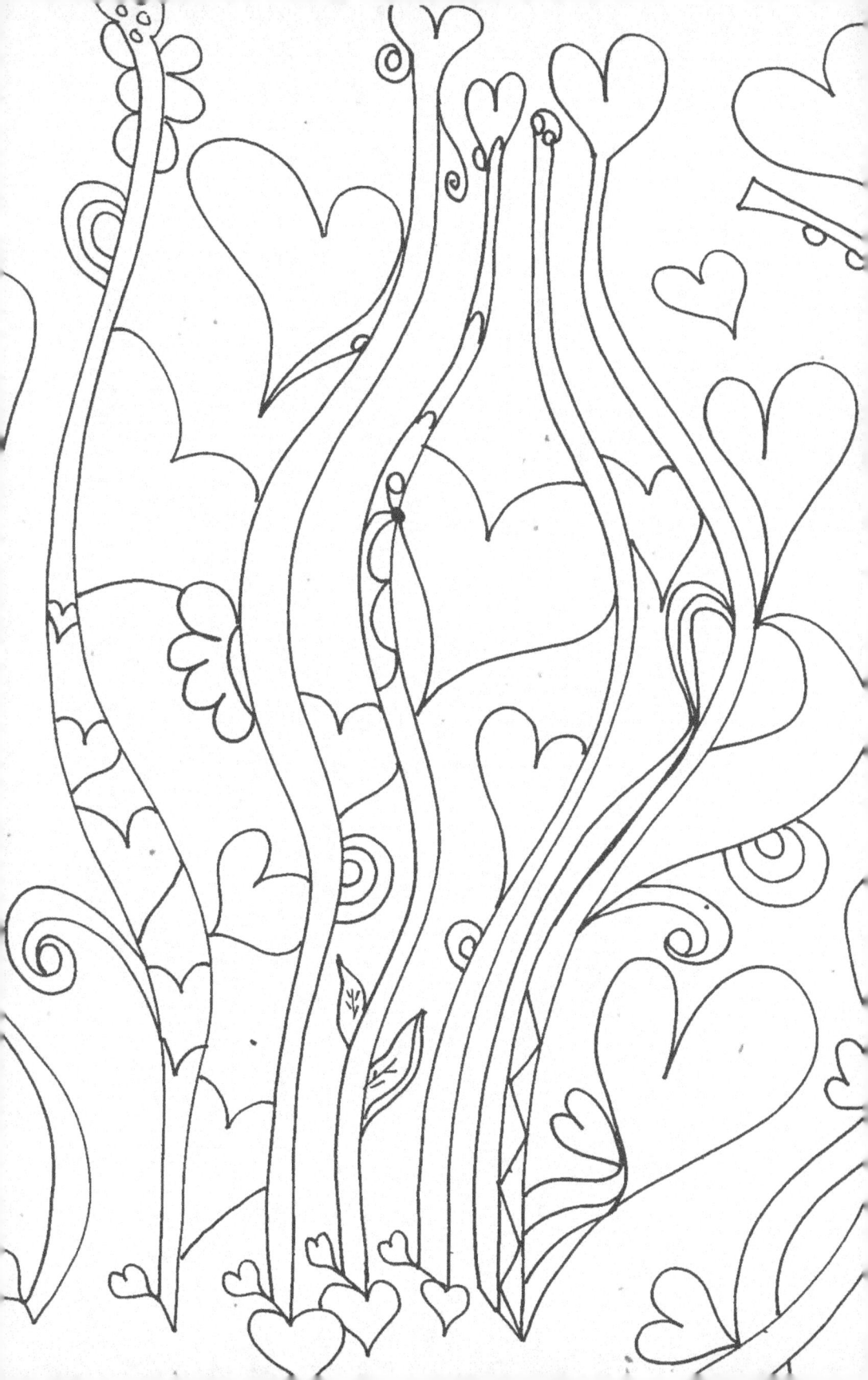

Growing....

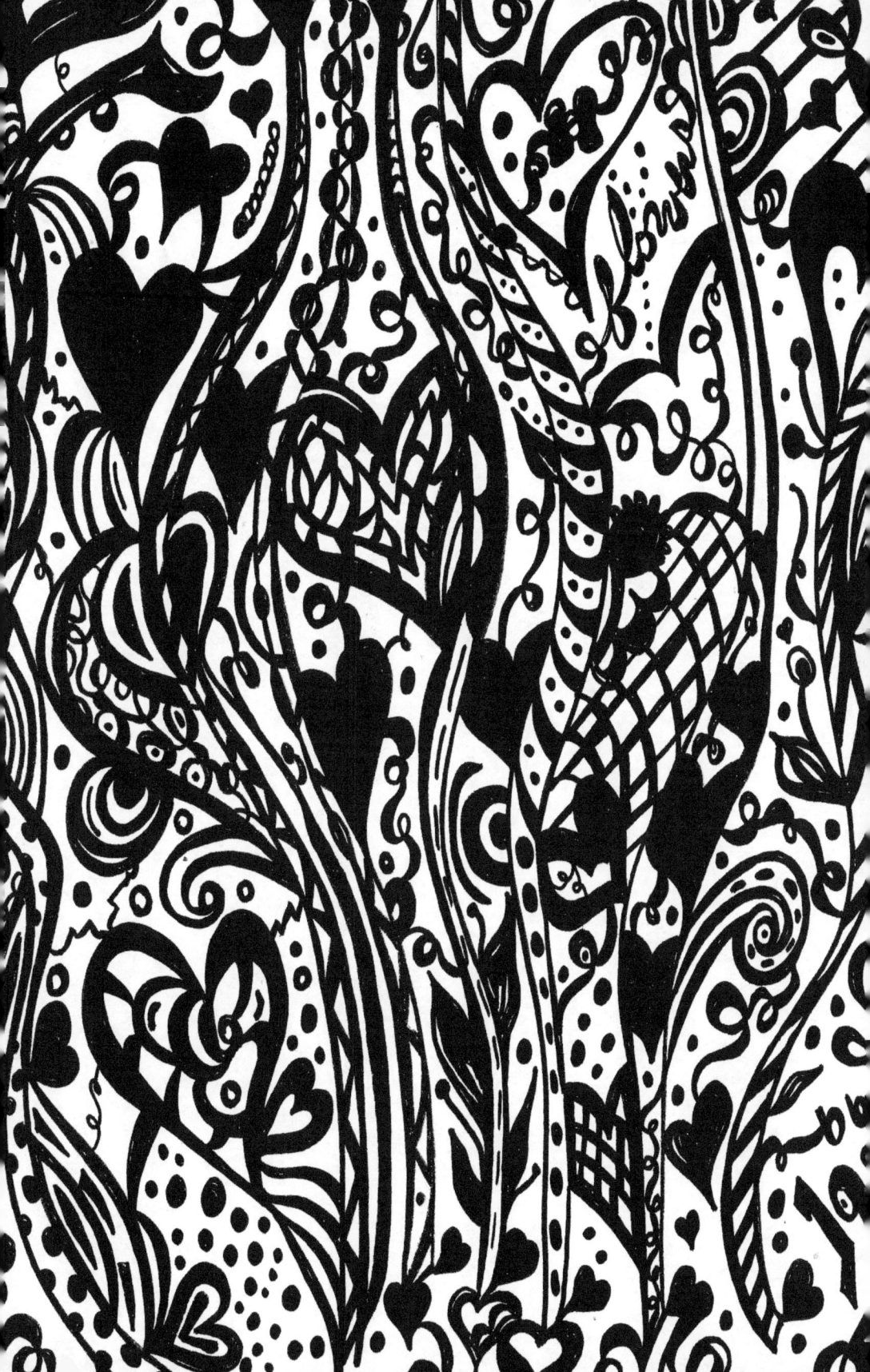

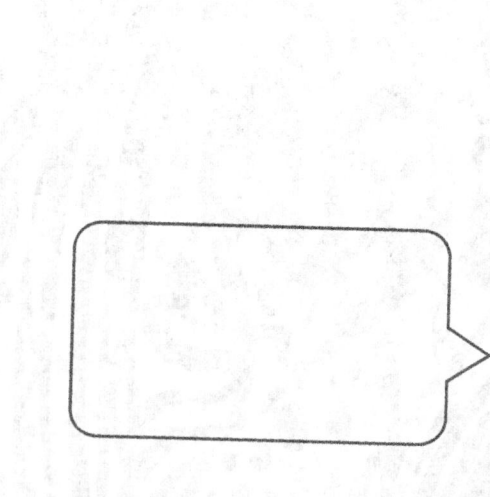

www.ingramcontent.com/pod-product-compliance
Lightning Source LLC
Chambersburg PA
CBHW061447180526
45170CB00004B/1598